COPYWRITING MASTERY

HOW TO SPICE UP YOUR WEBSITE SALES COPY AND WATCH YOUR SALES GROW

I0494358

ANTHONY EKANEM

Contents

Preface

If you are serious about succeeding in an online business, you must be ready to work hard to communicate with your buyers. If you are not prepared to put in the time and efforts needed to make your website stand out, then you need to take a serious look at your motivation for being in business in the first place.

Being online has some cache, but it also requires hard work, lots of research, time and a dedication to providing your site visitors with not only what they want but also excellent customer service. If you do not provide these or you are not available to answer their questions, do not provide fresh contents. And what is the point of having a website if your product does not sell?

Before you can be successful in building a business and be a success in communicating, you need to learn. You need the right attitude to grow your business and to deliver; there are no two ways about it. That would involve attitude, your attitude! You know if you talk to an upbeat, positive person, you come away feeling great yourself. The positive was communicated positively. On the other hand, if you speak to someone with a bad attitude, you will go away feeling grumpy and stressed.

You cannot communicate positively if you have an attitude problem. As weird as this might sound, your attitude and choice of words can directly affect the way you write your website copy. And if your attitude is not right, people reading your website copy will know that something is wrong somewhere.

Another thing you must have is a personal Mission Statement. And why do you need a personal mission statement? Because if you do not know what your mission is, how do you expect your potential customers to know? When crafting your Mission Statement, there some things you need to include, such as why your business exists, whether it provides products or services people want or need. Your mission statement will also include who your customers will be and why they will be better off doing business with you.

Identifying Your Audience Is Power!

With a mission statement fixed firmly in your mind (and displayed where you see it every time), you need to figure out what your market potential is and then know it inside-out. You choose your product or service because you feel it appeals to people.

Do you know the reason it appeals to other people and not only you? If not, find out fast. How will it benefit them? You need to know these things to talk to your market. This is vital because the bigger your market, the broader your target markets would become. The broader your target market, the better the growth of your business.

To understand how vast your market potential could be, you must know what your product or service offers to people and how it will benefit them. If you sell, for instance, weight-loss products, you will know instantly that virtually everyone is concerned about their weight. The weight loss industry is booming. You can market your product or service to anyone anywhere, regardless of age or geographical location.

Do not kid yourself about your market either; you will need to work your market to succeed. You will need to invest time, and money, into making sure you have up-to-date training and product knowledge. You will need to be committed to your product or service. Your online business is like any other "traditional" business, and you must work hard to succeed. Your product or service will not sell itself, nor will it generate income on its own. You must do those things to bring about a result. And if you do them surely and steadily, success will be yours.

The Tools You Need

As a marketer online, you need to know what you are doing, where you are going, and what to expect. You need to know how to find prospects and how to handle them. That sounds like a huge task. It is not if you have and use the right tools, the proper training, and act daily.

There are many tools you can use. Instant messengers – does not matter which one you choose – just make sure they are a significant part of your marketing strategy. Email is critical. A well-written email can work wonders. Use phone marketing even if you do not fancy it that much. One quick call to a sales prospect, inviting them to a special online weight loss seminar, says a lot about how committed you are to your customers.

If you use relationship marketing correctly, it will guarantee you loyal customers that you will keep. Article marketing is smart marketing. You provide well-written and relevant articles to other websites, blogs, and ezines for free. This sets you apart as an expert, gives you leads, increases traffic to your website, and improves search engine rankings.

Blogging and search engine optimisation (SEO), are two other tools. Blogging provides a platform to combine text, images, and links to other blogs and webpages about your business, product, or service. With a blog, you can post updates on what you are doing, what new additions you have made to your product or services, any specials sales, and even product photos.

SEO here means understanding what human visitors would search for, and to help match those visitors with websites offering what they are looking for. Pay careful attention to this segment because it is crucial to you when you come to write your website sales copy.

If your business is reliant on cold calls, referrals, instant messages, and emails, you will know the importance of having a good website copy. You learn about your prospect and their needs through your interactions with them and determine how your product can meet their needs. Then you market to those needs in a language that gets their attention.

Still on Identifying Your Audience

If someone had asked you why you decided to build a website, you would likely tell that is to let people know about your business. The best thing to do when planning and building a website is to aim at your targetted audience – the customers who need or want your product or service. Indeed, that could be anyone, especially if you are marketing weight loss products. However, it is highly unlikely a horse trainer is going to be interested in your products. So, you need to refine your focus.

Who visits your website? Prospects, existing customers as well as your friends, relatives, and your employees. Each of these people would be looking for different contents. The way your website sales copy is written will determine what the next step will be for each of these user groups.

If you want to generate sales, provide excellent customer service, and communicate your employees and investors. You **must** have a copy that moves them to action. We mentioned this earlier when we talked about knowing what your audience is searching for. There are two ways to find this out. The first way is to find out what people want and need. These are your internal sources. The answers would likely cover product specifications, pricing, availability, features, as well as the benefits of the product or service.

The other source is external. This includes surveys, site keywords, and search engine keyword data. This will reveal to you what your customers are searching for and how they are searching for it. Generally, this means you have website tracking software onboard on your website. It is a rich source of information for you if you have. It will tell you the search terms visitors used to find your contents online.

Once you know what your website visitors think is essential, you can write a copy to fulfil that need and layout your website to supply the need information. You can also use keyword research tools to achieve this. This will give you a slightly different view than website keyword data. It will provide you with a clear picture of how all users interested in your product or service will search for those products or services. Understand most of these searchers will not be landing on your website anytime soon. However, it gives you a good idea of the search terms and phrases used.

When people perform a search online, they are trying to solve a specific problem. Many people search by describing the desired outcome. For example, the use of words such as improved, higher, better, more; tells you the results the searchers want. Others will search for a specific service. Though the results of using search engine keyword research tools are impressive, they may not be as applicable to your website as website keyword data.

Finding Your Audience

About the only way you can find your audience is to figure out who is going to be reading what is on your website. To do that, you must understand your audience is (we are using the weight loss website as an example). So, this means you will be writing for people who are overweight and want to lose weight safely. Thus, already you have what their expectations are, which are to lose weight safely and speedily.

- **What does your audience bring to your writing?** They bring expectations of a website that can help them lose weight.
- **What will your audience benefit from your website?**You want them to take away reliable information on how to lose weight safely.

What you have here is the five W's.

1. **Who is your audience?**People who want to lose weight.

2. **What do you want your audience to know or do after reading your contents?**You want them to know they can lose weight safely, believe

they can do it, and feel motivated to do so.

3. **When will your audience read your content?**Any time they go online and access your contents.
4. **Where will they read your contents?**They will read it while at home, at work, in the library, or anywhere else they might be.

5. **Why will they read it?**They will read it because it is well-written and has useful information. They may also read it because they must read it or are interested in it for professional reasons or because they are personally interested in what you have to say.

Your contents would vary to suit your audience' needs. And that means your writing style and format will also vary. If you are writing on weight loss issues for Doctors, you will use some jargon. If you are writing for those who want to lose weight, you will provide informative content.

The level you write to your audience is something you must consider. You should aim your contents at those with high school education, but still give those with higher education the contents they are searching for. This is all in how you write the copy.

What do you want your website readers to know? This will determine your style and organisation and will tell you if you are going to write about information or ideas.

Why Words Still Make a Difference

Words make a difference because they can be used to invoke feelings, thoughts, images, and actions. They can appeal to people on various levels – the visual reader, the auditory reader or the kinesthetic reader. More than anything else in life, words are the one form of communication that can deliver what we want people to know. They can convey simple truths, complex issues, humour, and sorrow. Words are the all-and-all in the complex world of communications.

CHAPTER ONE

Copywriting Starters

Just what is copywriting? It is the writing that is intended to promote a person, opportunity, opinion, or idea. Since we are talking about websites, we assume the writing will be on a website. This will be referred to as search engine optimisation copy.

There are, of course, other mediums that use copywriting and copywriters – radio and television commercials, billboards, magazine, and newspaper advertisements. And the point behind writing a copy? It is specifically designed to entice, persuade, or motivate a listener, viewer, or reader to take action. That action could be anything from purchasing a product to subscribing to a newsletter, from trying a product sample to participating in a survey or poll. You can also use copywriting to convince a reader not to do something or not believe something.

What types of materials use copywriting? Body copy, slogan, headlines, direct mail, biggies, taglines, jingle lyrics, sluglines, captions, news releases, research and white papers, and the website contents. And it is just the tip of the iceberg too. Do not forget there are also things like print advertisements, mail order catalogues, brochures, postcards, and greeting cards. Copywriting is a good line of work if you are good at it, as you will always have jobs.

Copywriting, when used on websites, usually refers to the style or method of writing and wording contents that is slanted to achieve higher rankings with the search engines. This is called content writing, which means the proper placement and repetition of keywords and keyword phrases on a website.

At one time, writing contents for websites was a means of getting better rankings because the writing was targetted at the search engines. That is not the case any longer. Writing is now more targetted at human visitors than search engines. The trick about this type of copywriting is to produce fluent and readable copies for search engine optimisation purposes.

How Copywriting Came About

In a moment of serendipity, copywriting came about because search engines got fussier about the words that they used to crawl and rank pages. It did not much matter when things first got started with the Internet in 1996. You could fiddle a bit with your meta tags or use one simple but a powerful word to get a good ranking. It was not even much of an effort to put up a webpage and get the tag picked, submit it to the few engines there were at the time, and voila, you were in business. And, you could even get listed in Yahoo! Directory for free. This is not going to happen in the 21stcentury.

Back then, the gurus of search engine optimisation did not give any thought to whether your website converted visitors to sales or provided anyone with a return on their investment. How a website performed was up to the owner, not the person who wrote the tags. Now things have changed.

What happened was that companies left standing when the dotcom market went to heck in a handbasket realised that while they could get visitors to their website, they could not make them buy something. So, what then was the point of a website that did not sell anything? That became the famous million-dollar question. It eventually led search engine optimisation specialists and website owners to the conclusion that surfing and landing on a webpage did not equate to money spent. So, what had to happen to the website to convert visitors into sales customers?

That question was half of the equation. The other half was how do you get regular conversions and maintain a long-term high ranking in the search engines? The answer was through the judicious use of well-written, fresh, informative, keyword-rich texts explicitly aimed at search engines and your website prospects.

How Copywriting is Influencing Your Life

Daily, we are bombarded by copies for hundreds of items. On average, the human mind can retain up to seven thoughts at once, so if one or more of those thoughts is about a product, service, or opportunity; then you have been impacted by copywriting.

If you spend any time watching the television or listening to the radio, you would be inundated with commercials about every seven to ten minutes. You likely retain some of those commercials, especially if they touch on something that is of interest to you. Once again, you have been impacted by copywriting.

Surf the Internet a lot? Then you know how much advertising there is on the internet and likely read hundreds of ads a week about a variety of products, things to do, something to buy, and courses to take. Each of those adverts, in most instances, has been carefully written to make an impression on you. If you remember advertising you have seen, then it did its work. And, you have been impacted by copywriting.

Given the numerous advertisements we are all exposed to daily, it is a wonder we even remember any of them. And therein lies the rub – how to write something that captures people's attention; how to inform your customers of what you can offer them in a manner that will be remembered.

Selling the Benefits

To inform your customers about what you can offer them, you want to communicate your intentions, goods, and services to them. The way to accomplish that is through emotional response writing.

Emotional response writing is an email, newsletter, or sales letter written to persuade the reader to place an order, request more information, or even to show support for a product or service. It gently taps the reader on the shoulder to take a specific action. To do that, you make an offer to the reader, not an announcement. The letter or email needs to go to the right target audience, appeal to their wants or needs, and be useful and informative.

Calling your audience to take action (a call to action) means a sale of sorts – but a soft sale. It will also mean you will need supportive documentation, other flyers, and pamphlets since if you use a sales letter, it often does not do the entire job of selling for you.

Getting Started

You need to know your products and services inside-out. Nothing can take the place of your knowledge and how you present yourself to your prospects. You will need to have resources on hand in addition to what you know, things like online resources, advertisements, articles, newsletters, and books.

The next thing is to sort out the benefits from the features of your products, business, or service. What will the product do for the prospect that needs or wants it? What will they gain from buying the product or service? What is the unique selling point of your products, business, or service? A benefit is a specific outcome of a feature of your product or service. Benefits motivate people to act.

Before you start writing to tell people what you can offer them, you need to ask yourself some questions. For example, how am I going to market this product or service? Will you need other information or details to go along with your letter? What do you need? Who is your competition? How are they marketing their products? What benefits can you offer your customers that the competition cannot? How much do you want to spend on advertising? Are your marketing goals and hopes realistic? Who is your buyer? Why would your customers want to buy what you offer them? The most common reason is the fear of missing out on something important. Does your offer appeal to their emotions?

Get Ready to Write Your Email

You have enough character spaces for the headline or subject line when you start pulling your email together. The letter needs to tell your reader what it is about and make a promise what the item will do for your reader. You have about just a few seconds to hook your reader, so use your main selling points first and add the benefits with it.

EXAMPLE:

Imagine organic pet food that does not use wheat gluten or other additives. 100% money-back guarantee.

Use power words, and these are: free, proven, imagine, how to, fast, cheap, enjoy, now, learn, introducing,etc. Use them, but do not abuse them or keep repeating them indefinitely.

The main body of your message enlarges the theme and provides more details. It also shows how you will make good the promise you made on the headline. Your close or call to action urges the reader to take the next step you want them to take. If you cannot put two words together, talk to a copywriter. This is one letter you must not mess up, as your business' success depends on it.

Tell a story your reader can easily identify with, almost like a testimonial. Announce a new product, service, or business, maybe a one-of-a-kind event, or important news about your unique selling point.

Treat the reader as your equal. For example, if you are selling hair loss products and services, address your letter with *Dear Fellow Hair Loss Sufferer*. Look for an inspiring quote for your hair loss product: "*Product XYZgrow now has a NEW topical all-natural proven hair loss product that will promote new growth.*"

Start your letter by talking about a problem the reader has, one your product can solve. For example: *Fed up with hair loss products that do not work and cost too much? We have got a cheap solution – XYZgrow that will work for you.* If you use this approach, tell your reader a secret, or a piece of information that many people do not know. Product knowledge and research come in handy here.

You could add more to your mail but keep it short and to the point. The body of your message should be written in the same tone as your subject line. Quickly give details of your unique selling points. Point out the benefits right away. Do not leave it until the end, or you will lose them. Prove your benefits claim by using the extra information you have on hand. Be creative, challenging, descriptive and build to the call to action.

The Call to Action

This is where you ask the reader to do something, like order your product or service or join your membership business. Make it easy for them to contact you. Provide a contact form, a toll-free phone number, an email link, URL or blog, and make sure they work before you send the email. Close with thanks for their time and attention.

Many internet marketers "save the best for the last". For instance, if you order before XYZ date, you will get a free web banner. This kind of information is best put at the beginning of your letter, right after the unique selling point or benefits area. It provides an incentive for the reader to keep reading to find out the benefits.

Leaving the cost savings or free goodies until the end is a bribe. If you do not grab them with the first seven to ten seconds, and that means putting your heavy artillery in the opening, then you could lose them.

Before you send out your letters, you may need to find test readers. Ask them to tell you what they think is missing, how you could improve your offer, and if they would buy from you if they needed such a product or service.

CHAPTER TWO

It Is Not All About Sales

You might think since you are writing marketing letters, and trying to sell something, that your email is about sales. It is hoped you will get a sale from your email, but the primary point to the email is not about sales. It is about relationship marketing. So, you do not want to "sell" your customer. You should have a relationship with them first, and from there, the sales will follow if you do your relationship marketing the right way.

Why would focusing on existing customers be more profitable? If you are always spending money and resources to attract new customers, your profitability will suffer. You are not building a loyal base of people who stay with you. Called "churn", these people will not come back to you. The term for attempting to keep people and increase their loyalty is to your business is called "defensive marketing". Those who have already bought from you are the key to your continued business profitability. And if your website sales copy and other marketing tools sizzles, then those wallets are going to open frequently.

You can also see your customer's lifetime value as a long-term asset. And you value assets and treat them accordingly. Keep your customers happy, and they end up being loyal. Customer loyalty is worth a lot of money to your business since the cost of keeping an existing customer is only about ten per cent of the cost of getting a new one.

Your Customer's Needs and Wants

No one is the same as another person when they come to you for a product, service, or opportunity. Everyone needs something specifically for them. If you are marketing online, first start with communication and build a relationship with people. The methods are many, including email, instant messaging, community forums, blogging, and websites. You want to show them what you have to offer and get them to your website. That takes work. Once they are on your website (and reading the excellent copy you have), get their email address by giving something away instantly. The instant reward keeps them interested.

Provide quality information, well-written, and adequately researched. This adds credibility. If the copy is good and motivates people, this will often translate into programme registrations or signups for a newsletter or requests for product information or even orders. This is the beginning of your relationship. It is where you start your long-term relationship with your customer and offer value-added extras to their commitment to participate. Let them know how to get the best value and usage out of their purchases. This, more than anything else, will set you apart from your competition. This step ensures you word-of-mouth referrals and customer retention.

Finally, provide your customers with the tools or feeling of being a valued member of a "community". This turns them into your biggest promoters.

Your website can use web-based relationship marketing by using either open contents or premium contents. Open content means visitors can access everything on the website. Premium content is limited to people who have registered their email addresses or have bought something. Choose what works best before you write the copy for the content method you opt for and do not deviate from your plan.

Web-based relationship marketing means marketing person to person and not marketing a business to an individual. The distinction makes a difference because people will open your emails and read them rather than treat them as junk mails. This does not cost a lot of money, nor does it involve considerable risk. It is merely human-to-human communication, creating bonds with your existing customers, and generating referrals.

What the Customer Will Respond To

This is not for marketing purposes; it is serious stuff and needs a fair amount of research to determine what a customer will respond to. People are different, and they respond to things differently. That is what makes being human either a challenge or a blessing. So, where do you start? Well, the best place to start is with Neuro-Linguistic Programming (NLP). It is used in the marketing industry to write copy, and for good reasons.

Neuro-Linguistic Programming is about your brain, language, habits, and patterns. Neuro deals with how you process the thousands of pieces of information you receive daily. You can do that in five ways: seeing, hearing, touching, tasting, and smelling.

Linguistic deals with language – the seeing, hearing, touching, tasting, and smelling wordsyou use to recall something. Programming refers to your habits, patterns, programmes, and strategies.

Some of the most memorable advertisements you have read or responded to are advertisements written using NLP advertising language patterns. These are adverts that get you to picture what your life would be like after you have purchased a product or service. For example, imagine the look on your friends' faces when you tell them you have tickets to see David Beckham play at a soccer match! You will get a mental picture of what they will look like, or more precisely, see their expressions.

NLP advertising language patterns in online website copy are subtle but effective. The idea is to motivate readers to act because they can imagine doing something with the product or service you offer. Here are a few examples:

i. "You can see yourself wrapped in luxurious mink." Note the visual appeal.
ii. "You can imagine in great detail the sensuous pleasure a mink coat will give you." Note the visual and kinesthetic appeal.
iii. "You can see your friends going green with envy when they see your new mink coat." Note the visual appeal.

You can even use questions to pique interest, such as: "Can you imagine the looks you will get from your friends when they see your luxurious mink jacket?" Again, the visual component. But you get the idea. Use the language of the senses to tell people what they will see, hear, feel, smell, or taste. These senses can be used to picture the consequences of buying your product or service. You are telling customers what they will experience.

Use your "sensual" copy on your website in your headlines, subheads, testimonials, the signature you use on emails, on order pages, sign up forms, follow-up emails, blog posts, business cards, answering machines and voice mail.

CHAPTER THREE

Creating a Sales Copy That Sells (I)

You might think you already know what your customers need, or you would not be in the business you are doing. You think you can sell your widget to anyone. No, you cannot sell it to everyone. However, you could do well with a targetted sales campaign – meaning you have correctly identified your target customers. Research shows roughly 50% of the success of a sales campaign depends on the correct identification of the right target customers.

This means you must know who your customers are to be effective in marketing and sales – to write the right copy for those targets. You can do these in many ways, and one of the most obvious ones is to research your existing customer base. You would be looking for buying behaviour, motivators, and other customer attributes, such as when they buy, how much they spend, what brands they like, and so on. You could call this process data mining, and in some instances, you would want to farm this kind of work out to specialists.

Data mining is discovering unknown, actionable, and profitable information from large consolidated databases and using it to drive your marketing strategies. For instance, say you choose a customer base of those between the ages of 35 – 65 to market your widget. On average, about 1% of the customer base is responders. Responders are customers who will buy the product or service offered to them. So, a random email marketing campaign to say 100,000 customers will likely generate about 1,000 sales.

However, if you identified which customers are most likely to respond (using data mining), you could raise your response rate to maybe 1.5% and only have to email 66,666 people to get 1,000 sales. That is powerful software. A boon for your website marketing, as once you discover who you are marketing to, your copy can be tested and tailored accordingly.

Continuous market research is another method you can use to know your target customers. And you need to do this because customer's needs and wants are always changing. This must be done on an ongoing basis, and while expensive and time-consuming, it will pay high dividends when your sales take off. Once you know your target(s), you can start writing to them.

Other methods to identify your customer's needs are using current and lost customer interviews, focus groups, be your customer, customer feedback and complaint logs, and customer observation.

Addressing Customer Needs

This section is going to be short and sweet because once you know who you want to market to, addressing their needs is almost a snap. Put yourself in the role of being the customer. Ask yourself questions about what you would want if you were a customer wanting or needing your product. Would you want a warranty? Want the product in different colours? Want to try it on? Want a gift certificate? Want replacement parts? Want service help? Want technical support? Want a brand-new innovative product?

Now you have an idea of what your needs are, extrapolate this to other customers. And, even though every customer is different, they have many similar qualities you can "work" with. Above all else, quality customer service is the key to retaining loyal customers.

What you are doing when you address customer needs is offering them a solution to an unsatisfied want or need. If your product can fulfil an unmet need or want, you will have sales. It is up to you to present your customers with the "plan" to buy your product as a solution to fulfil their unsatisfied needs or wants. Write the right way, and you will have loyal customers.

CHAPTER FOUR

Creating a Sales Copy That Sells (II)

Here are five techniques that you can use for writing articles on the web which will help you to stand out among your competitors and improve your sales and marketing potential significantly. You can use these five techniques to improve your comparison-shopping portal that you have to help you with choosing the deal of your choice according to your taste and suitability of your budget.

These five writing techniques could be used prominently on an insurance website to highlight various features that people would have to choose from for their insurance needs and various situations. You could use these techniques to explain why they should not just buy a car insurance policy and then neglect them ending up costing them more money in the long run or even leaving them uninsured.

Using these five article-writing techniques will enable readers to understand that things and events that happen around us and impact on our lives happen for a purpose. Once we accept it happened for a reason, it is one of the keys to accepting there are things in our lives we do not have control over.

Dissecting the Copy or Burying It for Good

One of the most annoying things on the internet in terms of website copy is the run-on sentence. It goes on and on like the Ever-Ready Energizer Bunny! It never holds together, and if it does, you have to read it many times until you to get the point where you give up. Who has the patience to read copy three, four, five, or more lines long? No one. Add this with the fact that most internet-savvy surfers detest long pages with an information run and will lay down dust as they leave the offending website. Talk about a recipe for disaster. You want people to stay on your website and read the content and hopefully buy something. If your writing bites, they will not be buying, never mind staying.

Let us try taking apart, the BAD copy, paragraph by paragraph.

Paragraph One

Here are five techniques that you can use for writing articles on the web, which will help you to stand out among your competitors and improve your sales and marketing potential significantly.

Paragraph Two

You can use these five techniques to improve your comparison-shopping portal that you have to help you with choosing the deal of your choice according to your taste and suitability of your budget considerations.

Paragraph Three

These five writing techniques could be used prominently on an insurance site to highlight various features that people would have to choose from for their insurance needs and various situations. You could use these techniques to explain they should not just buy car and bike insurance policies and then neglect them ending up costing them more money in the long run or even leaving them uninsured.

Paragraph Four

Using these five article writing techniques will give readers an ability to understand that things and events that happen around us and impact on our lives happen for a purpose that we don't realise but that once we accept it happened for a reason, it is one of the keys to accepting there are things in our lives we don't have any control over.

Can you believe you have just read a seven-line sentence? What were they thinking? Can you make any sense of this long sentence? What does article writing have to do with accepting events that happen around us we have no control over? No real point to this sentence unless it is supposed to be a genuine mystery.

Paragraph Five

So, if you need a good website copy and want to get your site seen by lots of people, we can tell you how to do it because we have lots of stuff you can use. Just buy our programme, and you will see that the things we are telling you make sense, and you can learn lots.

SAMPLES OF GOOD SALES COPY

Well, you have got to admit the above bad sales copy was terrible. What we are going to do instead of re-write the whole thing as one related piece (because it is not!) is break each paragraph down and redo it.

Paragraph One BEFORE

Here are five techniques that you can use for writing articles on the web, which will help you to stand out among your competitors and improve your sales and marketing potential significantly.

Paragraph One AFTER

Give your competitors a run for their money with these five fail-proof writing techniques. Improve your website sales potential and marketability!

Paragraph Two BEFORE

You can use these five techniques to improve your comparison-shopping portal that you have to help you with choosing the deal of your choice according to your taste and suitability of your budget considerations.

Paragraph Two AFTER

These five techniques can improve the navigation factor of your comparison-shopping portal. Find deals to suit your tastes and budget!

Paragraph Three BEFORE

These five writing techniques could be used prominently on an insurance site to highlight various features that people would have to choose from for their insurance needs and various situations. You could use these techniques to explain they should not just buy car and bike insurance policies and then neglect them ending up costing them more money in the long run or even leaving them uninsured.

Paragraph Three AFTER

Discover what insurance coverage you need before you invest in it. Keep your insurance up to date or risk being unprotected when you most need it.

Paragraph Four BEFORE

Using these five article writing techniques will give readers an ability to understand that things and events that happen around us and impact on our lives happen for a purpose that we don't realise but that once we accept it happened for a reason, it is one of the keys to accepting there are things in our lives we don't have any control over.

Paragraph Four AFTER

Things and events that impact our lives happen for a reason, but that does not mean we have control over them.

Paragraph Five BEFORE

So, if you need a good website copy and want to get your site seen by lots of people, we can tell you how to do it because we have lots of stuff you can use. Just buy our programme, and you will see that the things we are telling you make sense, and you can learn lots.

Paragraph Five AFTER

Want a dynamic website copy? Discover the insider secrets to make your copy come alive. Investing in our software will teach you lots of tips, tricks, and techniques for writing a brilliant website copy.

Did you see the differences? Hear the differences? Feel the differences? Now try some on your own. Find a site that needs a re-write and see if you can zing it up.

CHAPTER FIVE

Techniques to Make Up Their Mind

It is good to know how the mind works so you can adjust your sales copy to appeal to specific mind sectors. Let us start with some basic information to give you a good idea of how the human mind works. The brain does two major things: it stores information in your memory and processes information that allows you to use or apply your knowledge to make decisions and solve problems. Next, we will look at what side of the brain does what.

The left brain works with logic, parts, words, specifics, analysis of situations in detail, and sequential thinking. The left brain has a sense of time and a sense of your goals correlated with your position about those goals. Talk about a finely tuned instrument. The left brain also governs or runs the right side of your body.

The right brain works with pictures, emotions, wholes, and how all the parts relate together, putting stuff together, and simultaneous or holistic thinking. This side of the brain does not wear a watch as the left side. The right side of the brain can lose track of time. The right side of the brain governs or runs the left side of the body.

Brain functions can be broken down even further into what each side of the brain does. So, let us look at what the left side does.

The left side of your brain deals with tasks like being logical, sequential, analytical, objective, focus and details, and numbers. So, if you are bad in mathematics, blame the left side of your brain – or the right for not governing the numbers part of you.

The right side of the brain deals with tasks like being intuitive. Trust your hunches. They are usually based on facts filed away just below the conscious level. It also deals with colours, rhythm, pictures, and is random.

We have heard about limited attention span, and in marketing, that sometimes appears to be the norm for many customers. What it means is that only a part of the memory can be triggered at any one time.

Repetition

You read earlier that people need to be told about a product or service at least seven times before they buy it. So, repetition is the key to making your product known. You do not have to be annoying about it but find creative ways to keep your message in front of your audience. If the means changing your website copy, pictures, specials, then do it and do it with something bordering on the obsessive. Always keep your main selling point as your focus.

Here is an example of what we mean, told in a short story. See what you remember about the story after you have read it.

Once upon a time, there was a cat named Charlie. Charlie was the most handsome cat in any farmyard for miles around. Charlie was so handsome that the local Veterinarian, Dr Roth fell madly in love with him. But Charlie, who was such a handsome man, though he was too handsome for Dr Roth. So, Charlie decided to join an acting company, run away from the farmyard and become the next Morris the Cat. Charlie knew his dreams would come true.

Try not to look back at the story. Can you recall the name of the Veterinarian? Maybe yes or no – but one thing is for sure, you remembered the cat's name because it was repeated six times. There is nothing like a 2x4 over the head. But you get the point, repetition sticks in the minds of your readers, listeners, or viewers.

Repeating things so often is not saying that your readers have faulty memories. It is just human nature that sometimes things need to be pounded into their heads. Remember, they (and you) can only think of one thing at a time.

Your website copy should not be as repetitive as the little story you just read. But you need to figure out your key selling point to hammer home to your customers. For example, if you are having a sale, you need to emphasise that. If, on the other hand, you want your name out there and get it known, you need to repeat that at least twice in anything you do.

Will people find your repetition annoying? If you mess up the writing job, yes, they will. But if you do a nice clean script with good flow and use the keywords in repetition in a smooth flowing way, they will not find it annoying. Another thing here would be to try and use keywords that are not complicated and convoluted. Keep it straight, clean, and simple.

You should also know that most people read websites with half an eye unless they are keenly interested in them or are looking for what you have. So, repetition in your site copy will stick with your readers later – kind of like subliminal messages. So, the bottom line is that repetition is one of the smartest marketing strategies you can use to get people to remember your name and message.

What if your website traffic is decent, you have adverts all over the internet and in lots of free classifieds? Will this be enough to make sales? The answer is no, it will not be enough, because there is no repetition.

People on the Internet are bombarded with thousands of advert messages daily. In most instances, we just hit the delete key and do not even read what the advert said. Or, they get caught in the spam filter. Do you remember every advert you saw when you surfed on the internet today? No? Well, no one else does either.

What you would remember is seeing the same message repeatedly. What you would likely recall, and more so if you are interested in the subject, are things like those free ten-day mini-courses. This is something you could consider for your website as well. The promotion for it would be done in your well-written copy that people cannot resist. Or they may resist the first few times, but after having seen what you are offering and having read the message several times, that would make up their minds.

That process usually goes like this. See the advert the first time and have no intention of buying the product or service. But they want the information you are offering for free about the product or service. They sign up.

Now you have an opt-in customer that you will send information to in instalments. You, of course, make sure the information in the mini-course is well scripted, fresh, useful, and informational – something people can make use of. You will offer people a full course as well, and you will provide your visitors with that information in each email. By this time, the customer has seen your name, message, and key selling points at least seven to ten times (depending on the length of your mini-course), and they figure it is a good product and – right, they buy it.

They bought it because they saw it for seven to ten weeks and were able to figure out or see your offer had good value; thanks to the information you sent them every week. By the end of the course, you have credibility with your customers. There are not many people that will buy a product on the

Internet the first time they see it (unless it is the last Harry Potter book). If you have an excellent product or service, stick to website marketing that sells – do it the right way and do not use a one-shot advert. Use the opt-in names you capture at your website and send them a free introduction course.

The bottom line here is to stay in regular touch and always have great information, tips, and news to share. Do your homework and know your customer's birthdays and the birthdays of their children. Understand their profession and what is of interest to them. You will become an inbox repetitive regular – you have successfully used relationship marketing to make sales.

Here is something else to consider, as well. By positively reinforcing the behaviour of your customers (the behaviour is visiting your website and buying), you will retain them as loyal customers.

In other words, a consequence (positive reward) is presented to your customers dependent on a behaviour (visiting your website and buying your product or service). Positive reinforcement can be as little as sending your customers something they will value highly in their line of work (and that could be killer information) or offering a mini-course that will change their outlook about your product or service.

You could also offer discounts, better buys on bulk purchases, to die for customer service that no one else can beat or a newsletter that has everyone talking because it is so good.

Other Techniques That Work Every Time

We have touched on Neuro-Linguistic Programming earlier in this book as we were talking about language patterns. This is an excellent tool or technique to have in your arsenal for writing sales copy. It gives you that edge over many other writers. If you have spent any time reading sales copy on the internet, then you already know what is and is not good. Sometimes that is intuitive, but mostly good copy screams good copy. Bad copy – well, it too speaks for itself, and guess what? Bad copy drives people away.

NLP language patterns have always been a long time. This came about as the consequence of research into why two people who have the same experiences react to them differently. Of course, you react differently, but that is not the point. The point is that not only are your reactions different, the language you use to describe your reactions is also different.

People then tell you how they perceive various circumstances using the language of their lead and backup system - auditory, visual, or kinesthetic.

This is not magic. If you pay close attention to what your customers are telling you – read the language they use, hear the language they use – you will know what lead systems they are using, and you can write your sales copy to suit their Neuro Linguistic patterns.

Here is another benefit to using your customers' language patterns, in emails, phone calls, notes, etc. Yes, and in sales copy. Roughly 96% of your customers will be visuals and will respond to those kinds of words that strike a visual chord (make them see something). If you use their language, you will be in sync with them and can use their system to communicate with them. In a world where it is hard to communicate with others and be understood, using Neuro-Linguistic language patterns is a bonus you can bank on.

CHAPTER SIX

How to Get Their Attention

Testimonials can give your website a boost if they are done the right way. If they are not, you could wind up driving traffic away in droves. Remember, the critical thing about testimonials is the fact that they must be credible. Do not fake sincerity because people will know it is false.

We have seen websites that had testimonials on them that seemed too good to be true with a lot of sales trigger words, and wholly unbelievable. No two ways about it, they came across as phoney. Bad move for you and your website.

Ask your customers and other people who have done business with you for a testimonial. Ask them for feedback and then include the best ones on your website. Do not write your testimonials or have someone else do them for you. What do they know about your product or service other than what you tell them? They have not experienced your product or service, so how valid do you think testimonials written by a hired writer will be?

You have likely seen website testimonials from so-called "satisfied customers" who only have initials. If they were all that satisfied with the product, why did they not stand up and say so?

Each testimonial you use must have your customer's full name and location. If they are speaking on your behalf, then include your company's name. If they possess any professional certifications, you can use them. This will give their comments more weight and authority. And if they have a website, include it. This will prove your testimonial is genuine.

If you can use pictures with your testimonials, do so. Use "real people" pictures, not stock photos. In other words, a photo that is not perfect will be believable, while the one that looks highly professional may not be. Such are the whims of internet users. Always ask your customers for permission to use their comments. Or you may find yourself in trouble later.

How about an example of a BAD testimonial vs a GOOD one?

First, the BAD:

"Your prices are unbelievable for the work you do." -Tim W., Washington

Of course, this faint praise comment could be read two ways and does not have the person's full name, although it does have a location. It could be taken that the prices charged are unbelievable for the work – meaning the work is overpriced and not all that good. You want to stay away from comments like this because ambiguity will kill your reputation.

Now the GOOD:

Our advertising agency went out of business a week before our awards banquet, leaving us with no menus, tickets, or programmes for over 200 expected guests. On extremely short notice, Spiritwriters came through for us with everything we needed at a reasonable price, and the design was tasteful and eye-catching. We will be using them for all our work in the future.

* *Nicollet Haraden, Owner and Founder of Small Business Women of America, New York.*

Now we are talking! This kind of testimonial will go miles for you on the internet with other customers. You can have testimonials on their page, or better still, thread them throughout the copy on the website. It is much more dynamic that way. And if you have them on the main pages woven in with your text, and in sidebars, there is a higher chance of having them read than if they are on a page by themselves. If your testimonials are focused and specific, this is a powerful technique to improve sales conversions by directing attention to the benefits of your product or service.

Remember, if you want your testimonials to do their job effectively, they have to be readable. No one reads the long ones anyway because they do not have time. What you do with long testimonials is break up the whole text into bites and scatter them throughout your website.

MONEY BACK GUARANTEES

Money-back guarantees fall into the category of risk reversal marketing, and they can if appropriately handled, increase the conversion rate on your website. Let us face it; most products or services come with a guarantee of some kind. And you use that guarantee on your website to make the customer feel safe, to say they will buy what you have to offer. What you want them to think is it is guaranteed to work or make me happy or get the results I expect!

Risk reversal marketing is smart marketing and came about because of marketers noticing people would not buy as much online due to the risk inherent in buying a pig in a poke. This, of course, would affect impulse buyers. When you purchase anything, you make a deal, and if you have no guarantee, the customer is taking all the risk if the product or service does not meet their expectations. Realising there had to be some give and take in the risk arena, online marketers started offering a money-back guarantee to capture more buyers.

With a money-back guarantee, the risk of buying is shifted back to the seller. Now having said this, there are many kinds of money-back guarantees. The best one is the one that lets you return a product with "no questions asked" or "for any reason" and gives you a gift to boot. Then there are the ones that say, "for the following reasons". This can get tricky because a customer might not like the product for a reason not listed. This is a way to limit risk, but it may boomerang on you if not handled properly.

A guarantee only has validity if the company offering it treats its customers the right way and backs their product 100%. To check that out, look for company reviews. The major problem with guarantees with conditions is customers find it hard to assess their buying risk. This risk doubles (to the customer) if they are not sure the company is reliable.

Also, keep in mind there are two lengths of guarantees: 15 days and 30 days. The ideal situation is a 30-day guarantee; it will give customers lots of time to try your product and see if it suits them. Also, with a 30-day guarantee, many people feel safer with having longer to decide about a purchase they made.

Give Them Numbers

What is more apt to capture your attention? Copywriting that says, "our product removes most blemishes in a short time" or "our product has been proven to remove 80% of facial blemishes in three days"? Obviously, the copy with the numbers is easier to understand and less vague. It also will get people's attention more. It sounds scientific and measurable, giving it an air of credibility.

When you are writing copy that sells, you want to be very specific about the benefits. Why should someone buy this product versus another product? How fast will the product work resolve their problem? How effective is the product in terms that are quantifiable and measurable? Do they know what to expect by the copy that you have written on the way the product works?

Another reason to give them numbers is that the human mind tends to quantify things in small units. It is easier to remember the benefits when they are listed out in percentages or day intervals that can be applied to a person's frame of reference. You can even make it more appealing by using number metaphors that help them to understand exactly how wonderful your product is.

For instance, say you are selling tax preparation software to people who are trying to file their taxes by a specific date. What are the benefits? Is it the fact that the taxes can be done automatically? No! They can hire a tax preparer to do it for them. You have to offer the benefits in terms that people understand. You might suggest:

Ninety-five per cent of people using XXXsoftware received their refund within three days. Over 75% of people increased their refund, some even by as much as $2,000.

It is obvious to see why this software would appeal to the average tax preparer who may be wanting to increase their refund or get it quickly deposited in their bank account without going to a tax preparer.

Many large companies sell their benefits this way. McDonald's does not specially say, "We sell hamburgers." We know they do that. They say:" Over 99 billion served." That tells you that their hamburgers are so yummy that they fly off the shelves.

Limit the Time Available

Limiting the time your offer is available is another smart business move. And it can be a good motivator for people visiting your website to buy – NOW! Why? Sometimes it is the things you do not buy you regret more than the ones you purchase. So says a study to be found in the Journal of Consumer Research, which looks at how limited time offers affect spending behaviours.

The study examined how narrow windows of opportunity affect the spending habits of people. When consumers choose not to buy an item, they often experience feelings of regret.

The author suggested that selling cues such as "three-week sale" or "limited opportunity" tend to heighten the urge to spend and tie into the need to avert regret over **not** buying an item. This is due to the idea that one has to seize the opportunity when it arises or face a loss of that opportunity. Loss of capital or money is not as apparent in a buying decision as much as the satisfaction of a need met.

Everyone likes to brag about a great deal they snagged on a perfect sale, but no one likes to talk about the deals that got away. This is basic investment psychology of people that are risk-averse more from not doing something than from doing something. So, ask your visitors to do something. Ask them to buy in your call to action and limit the time when they can get that great deal. This pushes those buttons that will give you some extra moments of browsing that might be the difference between a sale and no sale.

Just do not do like some websites that limit an offer, and then after that offer is supposed to be over, it suddenly is extended. Consumers may act on automatic responses, but they are not stupid. There are furniture liquidation warehouses that have "final sales" repeatedly. At some point, they lose all their credibility with their existing customers and must always search for new ones to make up the difference. Your loyal customers are a goldmine, do not abuse them.

CHAPTER SEVEN

Drawing Them In

A sales copy is only useful if someone reads it. You can have the best team of writers doing your website, and you are getting a few visitors. Few visitors equate to poor sales. So, what do you do to draw people to your website? You have to entice them to move from a high traffic area on the internet to your website. Remember that if your copy is dynamic and influential, it will draw people to your website. It must first be exposed to an audience.

Search Engine Optimisation(SEO)

As discussed earlier, search engine optimisation (SEO) used to be the standard whereby copy was used to generate visitors through search engines. It is still a good strategy and can be helpful to a website in getting better exposure. However, now there are other social networking strategies that you can use that can be just as effective at improving your search engine placement and attracting visitors at the same time. So, do not trash SEO, but remember to add your copy to social networking sites where people congregate and are ready to browse.

Article Directories

Before we go into the social networking areas, let us talk about article directories. We discussed email and text marketing. These are effective strategies for people who have already signed up on your website. However, where will you get the new visitors to come from?

Here is where article directories can help in giving your website a more prominent exposure. You can have a copywriter to write something relevant to your product that provides people with great content and directs them for more at your website. The article is posted on free article directories that are often distributed to many different people looking for new and interesting content that they can use on their websites.

This copy is not a hard sell; it would not even be classified as a soft sell. It is merely a link generator. You are generating outside links with significant traffic to your website, which may still be growing. You can mention your product as part of the article, but it should not read like an infomercial. Instead, it should seek to be engaging, informative, and fun. It should make the reader want to click on the link included in the author byline, which should be sending them to your website.

You should make the article free to distribute only on the condition that your byline and link goes with it. This can turn into a very viral form of advertising, which can generate a lot of traffic if your copy is good.

Social Networking

There are places like Facebook and LinkedIn that are social networking websites. These sites create a web of people who network with one other. They can expand your network of business contacts or create a very friendly venue where you can reach out to customers on a virtual face-to-face venue.

Once you start making friends, their networks lead you to other contacts of people who have a similar interest to what your website is about. It creates relationships that can turn into loyal customers. It can help you team up with people who have products that complement your own. Most importantly, to use a social networking site correctly, what you should do is to create a positive "buzz" about your product or product.

Buzz Is What Is Hot

Buzz is the byword that is used to denote the excitement and online trail of viral activity that makes a product or service appear personal, genuine, and a hot commodity. It is not viral marketing of a sales copy. It relies on getting people to talk to one other, on a one-to-one basis, to generate excitement for a product or service based on those relationships. Ideally, it is an electronic word-of-mouth campaign picked up and promoted by the people on social networking sites. It is not supposed to be about marketing a brand to people and creating hype when no one even cares about the product or is talking about it.

So, how do you get people to think your product is hot? Is there anything you can do to influence people's opinions and create buzz? Again, that is where your copy is going to come in. You want a copy that influences people's behaviour, and that is so dynamic that they want to spread it to the next person in glowing terms. On the internet, words are what sell, and if you are creating buzz, it is because your copy is catchy, and people find it personable.

Target Potential Buyers

While it may be fun to elbow up to the in-crowd, you are not there to be sociable. You are there to get exposure for your website and to convince some friends to become buyers, hopefully. Like the Tupperware lady that sells to her close group of friends and invites them over for Tupperware parties, you also need to know who you think might be willing to check out your website and products. You do not want to go into a social networking site and talk to people who want to buy a car, and you are a realtor. This would not be a good use of time.

So, you not only need to get a profile set up on the social networking site that identifies your speciality but also, you need to identify groups within the social networking sites that have your shared interests. This saves a lot of time marketing to people who are not interested. You want to know where your niche group is and spend your time there online.

Your Social Sales Pitch

By now, you probably are getting the idea that social networking is a little more sophisticated than plain sales copy. You are right! If you go to a social networking site or group and try to put in your best sales copy to generate interest, you will probably be flagged as a spammer. No one likes a spammer, and few people will bother checking out a product promoted by a spammer. You have to be more sophisticated than just joining a social networking site and copying ads from your website to introduce yourself and your product in this area. Instead, you have to focus on the relationship first and know when the opportunities for your sales pitch can arise.

Do you know how you are going to make a sales pitch without having to initiate the conversation first? It is very simple. Become the expert in an area that people are interested in that is relevant to your product or service. You are there to be an expert, not to sell things. Your profile should be professional, and it should reek of "expert" consultant. If being the expert includes recommending your products, then you have snuck in your sales pitch.

That is one way to use social networking to generate sales leads. There are others. Maybe you are selling fun products for parties. Then, you can develop an online persona that is fun to be around. You can always include your signature on postings that point to your website that show you do fun for a living. This is perfectly acceptable and not considered spammy. Always add a signature to any postings you do in social networking sites that point to your website to get the buyers from that site to yours.

Different Media for Different Websites

Some of the fun and intricate part of social networking is that not every website uses the written word as their way to network. Some places are for video fans. YouTube is excellent for video clips, and you will have to know how to create your video to join and be considered part of the social group.

Social Networking Controversy

One of the controversies of using social networking sites as a forum to sell your products is that this will detract from the geniuses of a referral. If too many advertisers find they are successful at generating buzz, the genuine buzz becomes hype, and it is no longer effective at selling anything. Just like emails that flood our inboxes and are now swiftly dispatched upon arrival, without ever being opened, if social networking buzz becomes hype, then it will die from its success.

CHAPTER EIGHT

Finishing the Sale and Beyond

Are you sweating yet? Writing great a copy almost seems easier than attracting people to your website. It can be tough to wait for traffic to increase on your website, but it eventually will with these techniques. If you have trouble generating visitors to your website to read your copy, then check out companies that will help you to boost visitors using their advertising schemes. They are not that expensive when compared to the time and energy expenditure of social networking sites.

Let us assume your visitors are streaming to your website now on a steady basis. Do you know how you will hook them and convert them from visitors to buyers? You must have a plan before you get the traffic because many people will visit a website once and be gone never to return. If you have not hooked them in within that first brief initial visit, the odds are that you are not going to see them back at your website again.

Gone Fishing

Now is the time to go fishing! You must bait your hook and cast it in the waters. You should have something for your visitor the moment they get to your website. The copy has got them there, and it may even have kept them there, but unless you put a nice, juicy worm on that hook, they are sure to be off on their way upstream to mate with some other lucky vendors.

What can you offer your visitors without banging them over the head with your product? More copies! People who are on the Internet are looking for useful information. They may have gotten to your website through a search engine. They may have gotten there because of something you said in a social networking group. They may have gotten there through buzz. However, they got there, something you said, directly or indirectly, piqued their interest. Why not satisfy that interest right away and get your foot in the door?

Always have on your website an area that asks your visitors to sign up for a freebie. It can be a free report, free newsletter, or a free tip sheet on something relevant to your website. It can be a free coupon. It can be free alerts on environmental factors if you sell allergy medication. It can be anything you think your visitor can use and would sign up for if all they had to do was give you their email address. Do not ask them for any other piece of information for now. You are not selling them anything at this point. You are hooking them into a relationship with you.

Do you remember when you were dating? Who did you like the best? Was it the man or woman who talked all about themselves and told you how wonderful they were? Or, was it the man or woman who listened to your needs and tried to get to know you better? Well, you, as the website owner, are that suitor. You must build that relationship first and work on getting the sale through the techniques we have described in this book. In short, the hard sell is more of a turn-off than it is useful.

Autorespond Like You Are There

Hopefully, the visitor will give you their email address, and now you have got them in the net, even if they are not quite in your boat yet. This is where you will want to have developed a series of great autoresponders.

Thank Them for Their Visit

The first autoresponder should thank them for their visit and assure them that their freebie is going to be delivered shortly to the email address they have provided. Assure them at the end that the email address will not be sold if it really will not be sold later on. Within this autoresponder, you can ask them to retake an action. If you have sent them an excellent report, you can tell them how the report relates to some products that you have and ask them to check out the latest deals or explain a limited time promotion for being a new member. Ask them to view other related products on your website or even make a purchase. Once they have a freebie, and you have their email address, it is now time to negotiate a sale.

However, do not expect them to buy right away. As we discussed earlier, they will need to see some repetition of the information to decide to buy. Just make it clear that now they are in the sales loop, and should they need more information, you are the expert that can help.

Include in whatever freebie that you sent via email or sales copy that advertises other products and services. Always take the time to inform your visitors what is being offered for sale. What might be complementary to the information they have requested, and ask for feedback.

Request Feedback

When you request feedback, you are the gentle suitor who reaches over the table and grabs a person's hand and stares deep into your date's eyes. This serves two purposes. It establishes a relationship, and it gives you an idea of which products your visitors are looking for and how you can gear your market to serve them better. The best feedback form will offer another freebie to entice them to fill out a short feedback form. You can then ask them what brought them to your website, what products they are interested in, and any timeframe they might have for buying. Also, leave a space for personal comments that can help you decide if new products need to be added to generate sales or if your customer service is not up to par.

More Autoresponders

Every time a visitor sends an email, posts feedback, or buys something, you should autorespond and take that opportunity to thank them and get them more acquainted with your website and services. You can even schedule weekly emails to go out with helpful tips. You can use a monthly newsletter to keep in contact with people on your website and remind them to visit again! Always seek to have a copy sent to people who visited you. They are your strongest potentials for becoming paying customers. Do not bug them too much, and if they request to be removed from a list, do so. However, it should be clear when they sign up that they are signing up to be contacted with new offers.

Ask for The Sale

Always ask for the sale in your autoresponders. Sell the benefits, but also get that call to action in there. You do not want the visitor to ignore the entire email because it did not ask for them to buy something. The limited time offer works very well here because of the risk-aversion of not buying something and later regretting it. You can say something like: "Only 24 hours before this offer expires."

Use the surefire ways to get their attention and close the sale. Place yourself in their shoes and think of all the obstacles they might raise for not buying your product and address them. Offer them a variety of options for payment methods so they cannot opt out at the last minute because they do not have PayPal, or they have to send a money order. Offering a secure online way to purchase your product is necessary to generate good online sales.

Did You Make a Sale?

Whether you made a sale or not, you can use either information to fine-tune your marketing strategy. If you made a sale, something about your copy, your marketing plan, and how you presented things was effective. Do you know what part of your strategy worked? How about all those people who visited your website and did not sign up or eventually buy? Do you know why they did not buy?

You have to create a very rigid sales pipeline. You want to know what is working and what is not working so that you do not spend time fixing things that are not broken while the basement is flooding. So, your sales pipeline should be able to track who showed up to your website, from where they came, what pages they visited, how long they were there if they signed up, and how many times were they contacted before they bought, or did they ever buy? These are all vital pieces of information for the long-term health of your online business.

Tracking Visitors

Your website should come with an area that is usually known as an administration panel. It should allow you to see how many visitors are coming into your website and where they are coming from. It should also show you which pages on your website are accessed more and how long people spent on your website. It should show you the number of unique visitors in a month and whether the trend is increasing or decreasing. It will even split it up based on countries and other factors.

If you want to get more data about the demographics of your visitors, you can always include that in your feedback form. Remember, we told you in the beginning that you have to identify your audience. Well, this is one way to do that. You want your copy to be aimed at the market that is interested in your products and services, and you want them to open their wallets.

You will want to know which copy is attracting more visitors. If you find one page on your website gets an enormous amount of attention, you will want to post links to relevant products and expand that area. This will help you to remove areas that do not work well and focus on those areas that are bringing in eyeballs and potential buyers.

Lastly, you can see where people came from. Maybe they found your free article on the article directory, and they are coming from that area. Then, you know that you should post more free articles and aim your energies there. If you see a few referrals from a website you spent a lot of time on developing links, you can cut your losses short and not continue to focus energies there.

Tracking the Sales Lifecycle

Once the visitor is there, how many of them converted to members and signed up to receive a freebie? This is very crucial information. If they are not willing to get their name on your email list, they are likely not going to turn into buyers.

You want to be very effective at converting web surfers into interested participants on your website. If your conversion rate is low, then you need to change the freebie and amp up your sales copy. This is the opening to your pipeline. If they do not enter, you do not make a sale.

Once you have them in the pipeline, you should know precisely how they will be marketed and what products you are going to promote in each email autoresponder or freebie. This can build a database of valuable information on what autoresponders are more successful than others. If you are losing people, then you will want to know in what part of the lifecycle of freebies, autoresponders, and special offers you lost them. Either way, this is valuable information. You will know precisely what is working and what is not working.

If your pipeline is not very well built, you will not know what part of your website or product promotions are successful and which are not. Of course, total sales will give you a great idea of how successful a product or service is, but do you know at what point in the marketing cycle that product was offered? If you are getting more sales in the initial stages of the pipeline, then you know that this is an effective area. You can then concentrate on building sales at the end of the pipeline by adding complementary services and goods.

CHAPTER NINE

Sales Copy Made Easier

Writing a sales copy is not all about content. It is also about presentation. If you picked up a brochure on a table and all you saw was one giant paragraph, odds are you would put it right back without reading it much. In this multimedia age, people expect to be fed information in a way that is so easily digestible that it has almost been "pre-chewed" for them. That means they do not want a copy that is too hard to decipher, that is hard to read, or that makes them tired after they are done reading it.

Here are some simple presentation skills that you should use in all your sales copies to help your copy jump out of the page, grab the reader's attention, all the while they are being fed the most important benefits of your product or service.

Pay Attention to White Space

Your webpage or paper is your canvas. You do not want to fill every space of your canvas with words. Leave some white spaces for your reader to appreciate. This serves two purposes. One, it is visually appealing. And secondly, it is less tiring on the eyes. If you have very little white space, what ends up happening is that your copy looks cluttered and too difficult to wade through. This may seem trivial, but it is one of the most important pieces of information on good webpage design and copywriting.

In this age of multitasking and digitised communications, having to wade through a lot of copy to get a message across is too much work for many people, especially those who are busy. You do not know when the visitor is finding your website. It could be while they were on their lunch break at work. They might have stumbled on it from a search engine. They might even have had a friend tell them about it on a social networking site.

The odds are that they are not going to give you more than three minutes to make a good impression. If that first impression is one of clutter and disorganisation, you will have lost a visitor potentially before they have even read a single word.

Grouping and Emphasis

If you want to add white space without ruining your copy, there are several ways to do it. The most obvious is to write a copy that sells the benefits in bulleted lists.

Look at the following two examples.

Introductory Paragraph One

Welcome to our website! We are selling organic products that we think you will love. We are committed to bringing you the most natural products from around the world and making it easy for you to shop for them in the comfort of your own home. Look through our great selection of health and beauty products to find something right for you.

What do you think? Boring. Not only dull, but it was a cliché from the get-go. How many sites have you gotten to that say welcome to our website? Do you see how the first paragraph talks about the company but in such vague terms and in one continuous monologue that is asking you to lose interest? Let us try it again.

Introductory Paragraph Two
100% Certified Organic Products from Around the World
We proudly offer:

- **Unique** and **practical**products to improve your health
- **Quality**products that bring out your natural inner beauty
- Over 20,000 items in stock from 15 different countries
- Money-back guarantee
- Free shipping on orders above $50

Do you see the difference here? You have sold the benefits of your website offers. You did it in fewer words than the first paragraph, and you did it with ample white space. Bullets and lists are perfect for this.

This example should prove to you that grouping your information in bulleted lists could have a dramatic effect on the presentation and communication therein. In this world of byte-sized operations, people are used to getting things this way. They do not want to have to dig through a large amount of copy to find out what you are selling and what makes it unique.

If you paid close attention to this example, you would also notice that some words were bolded. This type of visual emphasis can also drill in your benefits without having to add more words.

You can also use different fonts, underlining, and other types of visual effects to make some words have higher memory stickiness than other words. This is not only useful for getting your point across to people, but some search engines even add some weighting to words that have been bolded and underlined.

So, be very careful about how you decide to create emphasis. There are traditional areas where the emphasis is given, like titles and paragraph headings.

Titles and Headings

In web copy, it is sometimes permissible to separate larger paragraphs into two smaller paragraphs, even though they are on the same theme. The reason is that you do not want your page to look like one giant paragraph, and website space is more at a premium, which brings us to another point about white space. The first three inches at the top of your webpage are the most visible on every computer platform. This is the space to capture people's attention. Do not waste it with an advertising banner unless you are getting paid good money to do so.

You Do Not Have to Get Fancy

You have probably seen those elaborate webpages that open into a multimedia presentation. They are great if you have a modern computer. Otherwise, you may be shooting yourself in the foot. You do not have to get fancy to get someone's attention, especially if that someone is still using a modem line and will not appreciate the film you uploaded to your website. It will most likely make their computer freeze.

If you want to reach the widest audience possible, stick with words. You do not need to have sound on the machine to read a text message. You do not have to download RealPlayer or any other fine little piece of software to open your webpage. You do not have to crash out of your website and re-boot your machine when all you have presented there is pure text. If some of the videos and multimedia software things enhance your website, it is still a good idea to put a link and warn people that they are opening something in a different format.

Include Graphics

You can include graphics to spice up your sales copy. Graphs are perfect to indicate how a product is effective or saves money. Pictures are compelling communicators, just like words. Use them sparingly and make sure they do not drag to load. Whether your copy is on a webpage or a piece of paper, make sure to intersperse the graphics at reasonable intervals. You do not want to overload a page and make it too cluttered, and you do not want it to be so unattractive and straightforward that it does not grab anyone's attention.

The charts or graphs can be excellent for compressing a large amount of information into a relatively small space. It can make your products appear to be scientifically tested and give an analytical bent to your image. They do need to be supplemented with text that supports the image, but that is also not long-winded or complicated.

Graphics are handled differently from texts in a search engine. If you have information that you want a search engine to pick up, make sure you add text so that it is written in a copy. Also, do not use graphics to get better lettering or an original font. If it is a graphic and not an actual font like Verdana, the search engines will skip over it for the most part. The text should always be written in a font that is easily readable to the reader and to search engines.

www.ingramcontent.com/pod-product-compliance
Lightning Source LLC
Chambersburg PA
CBHW061520180526
45171CB00001B/264